Green Grows the Holly

Medieval and Renaissance Christmas Carols

Arranged for Lap Harp

Suzanne Guldimann

WEST OF THE MOON BOOKS
Malibu, California

For my parents, with love.

Many, many thanks to Carolee, Heidi, and Terri,
and to Sylvia, for all of her help and guidance.

Published by West of the Moon Books
P.O. Box 6133, Malibu, California 90264
www.westofthemoon.org

Green Grows the Holly
Copyright © 1998 Suzanne Guldimann
Illustrations copyright © 1998 Suzanne Guldimann
Third, revised edition © 2023 Suzanne Guldimann

All rights reserved. This book may not be reproduced by any means,
whole or in part, without written permission from the publisher.

ISBN 978-1-7344601-8-6

Table of Contents

Introduction 4
A Babe is Born All of a Maid 5
Angelus ad Virginum 6
Besançon Carol 8
Corde Natus ex Parentis..10
Cutty Wren 12
Dadme Albricias, Hijos d'Eva 13
Friendly Beasts, The 14
From Heaven Above to Earth I Come 16
Green Grows the Holly 17
I Saw Three Ships..18
Joseph Dearest, Joseph Mine 20
Nous voici dans la ville 21
Nova! Nova! 22
Orientis Partibus 24
Past Three o' Clock..25
Personent Hodie...26
Riu, Riu, Chiu 28
Seven Joys of Mary 30
Song of the Ship 32
This Endris Night...34
To Drive the Cold Winter Away 36
Tomorrow Shall Be My Dancing Day..38
Veinticino de Deciembre 40
Whence Comes This Rush of Wings?...42
While By My Sheep...44
Notes on the Music...46

On Playing the Pieces

All of the pieces in this book can be played on a lap harp with a range of just two and a half octaves. They can also be played on a larger harp, or on flute, violin, guitar, or any melody instrument. On a small harp you will need to play an octave higher than the music is written, treating middle C as low C. On a larger harp you may wish to add some additional chords in the bass. To make the pieces easy to sing, as well as to play on smaller harps with limited sharping levers, I've arranged them all in the keys of C or G and their minors and modes. There are notes on the history and background of the pieces at the end of the book.

Introduction to the Revised Edition

Green Grows the Holly was written in a time before modern page layout and music notation software. Reconstructing it was a challenge, but one that was worth the effort. This was my first book. It remains close to my heart. The loved ones who taught me many of these carols when I was a child are no longer here to sing them, but the music lives on—an enduring legacy from one generation to the next.

By the height of the medieval period Christmas was celebrated with great feasting and pageantry. The Christmas season began with Advent, four weeks before Christmas and lasted until Epiphany, twelve days after. The eight days, or "Octave," between Christmas and the first day of the new year consisted almost entirely of feasts and processions. The tradition of caroling evolved with these festivities. There are examples of Christmas hymns from as early as the fourth century, but by the fourteenth century Christmas music had moved from the church to the streets. A carol, or carole, was originally a circular dance accompanied by song. We now use the term generally to refer to all Christmas music, whether it is a carole, a ballad, a hymn, or any of a number of other types of song.

Accurately dating early music can be a challenge. A traditional piece collected in the eighteenth or nineteenth century could well be hundreds of years older, but without an earlier manuscript it is impossible to know for certain. Often we have words but not music. Broadsides, inexpensively printed black-letter sheets popular in the sixteenth and seventeenth centuries, preserve a wealth of Christmas lyrics, but less often preserve the tunes. They advise the musician to: "Sing to 'Greensleeves,'" or "to the tune of 'Old Chestnut.'" Sometimes it is the music that survives and the lyrics that are lost, or rewritten. Sometimes a manuscript will come to light with music long forgotten or believed lost. And often Christmas songs have lasted in the folk tradition, sung from door to door to bring luck in the new year, down through centuries and long after they have faded from written records.

In the music of the Christmas season are the echoes of more than a thousand years of history. By playing this music, by keeping it alive, we join hands with both the past and the future.

> *Some say that ever 'gainst that season come*
> *Wherein our Saviour's birth is celebrated,*
> *The bird of dawning singeth all night long:*
> *And then, they say, no spirit dares stir abroad;*
> *The nights are wholesome; then no planets strike,*
> *No fairy takes, no witch hath power to charm,*
> *So hallow'd and so gracious is the time.*
>
> —William Shakespeare

A Babe Is Born All of a Maid

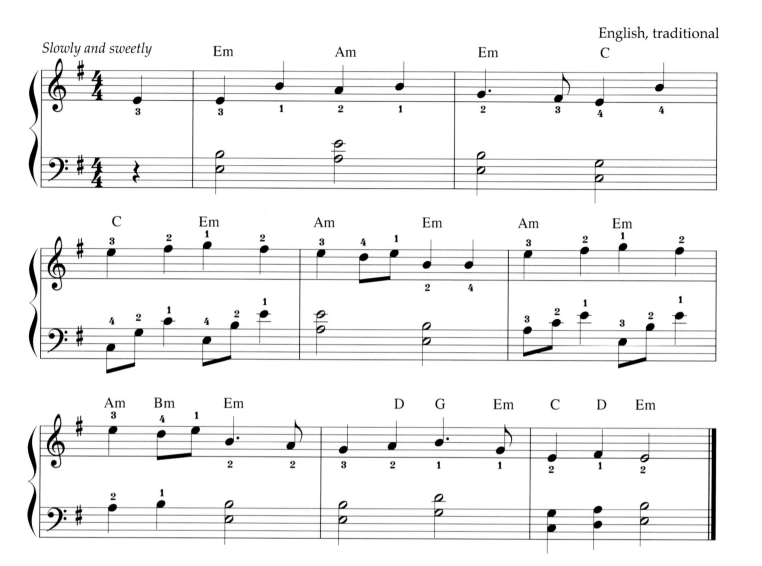

A Babe is born all of a maid,
To bring salvation unto us.
To Him we sing both night and day
Veni creator Spiritus.

At Bethlehem, that blessed place,
The Child of bliss now born He was,
And him to serve, God give us grace,
O lux beata Trinitas.

The Shepherds heard an angel's cry,
A merry song to them sung he.
"Why are ye so sore aghast?"
Jam ortus solis cardine.

There came three kings out of the East,
To worship the King that is so free,
With gold and myrrh and frankincense,
A solis ortus cardine.

The Angels came down with one cry,
A joyous song that night sung they
In worship of the Child:
Gloria tibi Domine.

—English, 15th Century

*Veni creator Spiritus—Come spirit of the creator
O lux beata Trinitas—Let light shine out of the darkness
Iam ortus solis cardine—Now the star of light has risen
A solis ortus cardine—Arise from the sun*

Angelus ad Virginum

Watch for lever changes

With Spirit

English, 13th Century

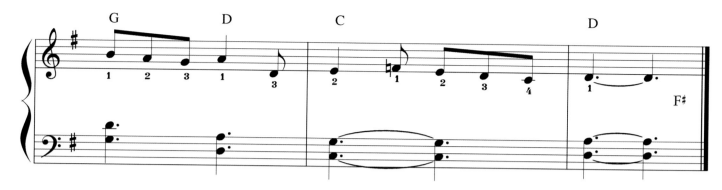

Gabriel, fram Heven-King	Gabriel, from Heaven's King
Sent to the maiden sweete,	Was sent to the maiden sweet.
Brought hir blisful tiding	Brought her blissful tidings
And fair he gan hir greete:	And fair he gave her greet:
Hail be thu, ful of grace aright!	"Hail be thou, full of grace aright!
For Godes Son, the Heven-Light,	For God's Son, the Heaven-Light,
For mannes love	For love of man
Will man become	Will man become
And take Fles of thee,	And take form from thee,
Maide bright,	Maid bright,
Manken fre for to maken	Mankind free for to make
Of sen and devles might.	Of sin and devils might."

Mildelich him gan andswere
The milde Maide thanne:
"Wichewise sold ich bere
A child withute manne?"
Th'angel hir seid:
"Ne dred tee nout;
Thurw th'Oligast
Sal been iwrout
This ilche thing
Warof tiding
Ich bringe;
Al manken wurth ibout
Thurw thine sweete childinge
And ut of pine ibrout.

Gently gave him answer,
The mild maid then:
"What way shall I bear
A child without a husband?"
The angel here said:
"Have no dread, fear not
Through the Holy Ghost
Shall this be wrought
This very thing
Whereof tidings
I bring;
All mankind's worth be brought
Through thine sweet child-bearing
And salvation wrought."

Wan the Maiden understood
And th'angels wordes herde,
Mildelich with milde mood,
To th'angel hie answerde:
"Ure Lords thewe maid iwis
Ich am, that heer aboven is;
Anentis me
Fulfurthed be Thi sawe
That ich, sith his wil is,
A maid, withute lawe,
Of moder have the blis."

When the maiden understood
And the angel's words were heard,
Mildly, with mild mood,
To the angel she answered:
"Our Lord, who is above, aye
His true bond-maid am I
Your words to me
This day fulfilled will be,
That I, since his will is this.
A maid, without [natural] law
Shall have a mother's bliss."

—Thirteenth century text from the Arundel MS,
possibly by Phillip the Chancellor (d. 1236).

Besançon Carol
Berger, secoue (Shepherd, Awake)

French, 16th Century

Berger, secoue ton sommeil profond!
Lévetoi et laisse tes moutons jouer!
Anges du ceil, chantant trés fort,
Apportez nous la grande nouvelle.
Berger, en choeur chantez Nöel!
O chantez, chantez Nöel!

Shepherd, shake off your drowsy sleep!
Rise and leave your silly sheep!
Angels from heaven are gladly singing,
Tidings of great joy are bringing.
Shepherd, the chorus come and swell!
O Sing Noel! Sing Noel!

Vois comme les fleurs s'ouvrent de nouveau,
Vois que la neige est rosée d'été,
Vois les étoiles brillent de nouveau,
Jetant leurs rayons les plus lumineux.
Berger, en choeur chantez Noël!
O chantez, chantez Noël!

Berger, levez-vous, hâtez-vous!
Allez chercher l"Enfant avant le jour.
Il est l'espoir de chaque nation,
Tous en lui trouveront la rédemption.
Berger, en choeur chantez Noël!
O chantez, chantez Noël!

See how the flowers open anew,
Thinking snow is summer's dew;
See the stars so brightly glowing,
All their brightest beams bestowing.
Shepherd, the chorus come and swell!
Sing Noel! O sing Noel!

Shepherds! Then up and quick away,
Seek the Babe ere break of day.
He is the hope of every nation,
All in him shall find salvation.
Shepherd, the chorus come and swell!
Sing Noel! O sing Noel!

—*French and English, traditional*

Corde Natus ex Parentis
Of the Father's Love Begotten

Piae Cantiones, 1582

Corde natus ex parentis Ante mundi exordium, Alpha et O cognominatus Ipse Fons et Clausula Omnium que sunt, fuerunt, Queque post futura sunt, *Seculorum seculis.*	Of the Father's love begotten Ere the worlds began to be, He is Alpha and Omega, He the Source, the Ending He Of the things that are, that have been, And that future years shall see, *Seculorum seculis.*
Ipse jusit et creata, Dixit ipse et facta sunt Terra, celum, fosa ponti, Trina rerum machina, Que que in his vigent sub alto Solis et lune globo, *Seculorum seculis.*	At his word all was created; He commanded, it was done: Earth and heaven, depths of ocean, In their threefold order one; All that grows beneath the shining Of the orbs of moon and sun. *Seculorum seculis.*
Corporis forman caduci, Membra morti obnoxia Induit, ne gens periret Primoplasti ex germine, Merserat quem Lex profundo Noxialis Tartaro *Seculorum seculis.*	He assumed a mortal body, Frail and feeble, doomed to die, That the race from dust created Might not perish utterly, Which the dreadful Law had sentenced In the depths of hell to lie. *Seculorum seculis.*
O beatus ille! Virgo cum puerpera Edidit nostram salutem Feta Sancto Spiritu, Et Puer, Redemptor Orbis, Os sacratum protulit *Seculorum seculis.*	O that birth, forever blesséd! When the Virgin, full of grace, By the Holy Ghost conceiving, Bore the saviour of our race, And the Child, world's Redeemer, First revealed his sacred face. *Seculorum seculis.*
Psallat altitudo celi, Psallite omnes angeli, Quidquid est virtutis usquam Psallat in laudem Dei! Nulla linguarum silecat, Vox et omnis consonet *Seculorum seculis.*	O ye heights of heaven, adore him! Angel hosts, his praises sing! Powers, dominions, bow before him, And extol your God and King! Let no tongue today be silent, Every voice in concert ring. *Seculorum seculis.*
—Aurelius Prudentius, 348-410	—English tr., John Neale, 1818-1866.

Note: the literal translation of the first line of the Latin version is "of the father's heart begotten." Seculorum seclis means "forever and ever."

The Cutty Wren
The Carmarthen Wren Song

Welsh, 15th Century

Dadme albricias, hijos d'Eva
Reward My Tidings, Sons of Eve

Spanish, 16th Century

The Friendly Beasts

English version of 12th C. French carol

Jesus our brother, kind and good,
Was humbly born in a stable rude,
And the friendly beasts around him stood;
Jesus our brother, kind and good.

"I," said the donkey, shaggy and brown,
"I carried His mother up hills and down;
I carried His mother to Bethlehem town."
"I," said the donkey, shaggy and brown.

"I," said the ox all white and red,
"I gave Him my manger for His bed,
I gave Him my hay to pillow His head."
"I," said the ox, all white and red.

"I," said the sheep with the curling horn,
"I gave Him my wool for His blanket warm,
He wore my coat on Christmas morn."
"I," said the sheep with the curling horn.

"I," said the dove, from the rafter high,
"I cooed Him to sleep that He should not cry.
We cooed Him to sleep, my mate and I."
"I," said the dove, from the rafters high.

Thus every beast by some good spell,
In the stable dark was glad to tell
Of the gift he gave Emmanuel,
The gift he gave Emmanuel.

—*Robert Davis (1881-1950)*

From Heaven Above to Earth I Come
Von Himmel Hoch da komm'ich her

German, 15th Century

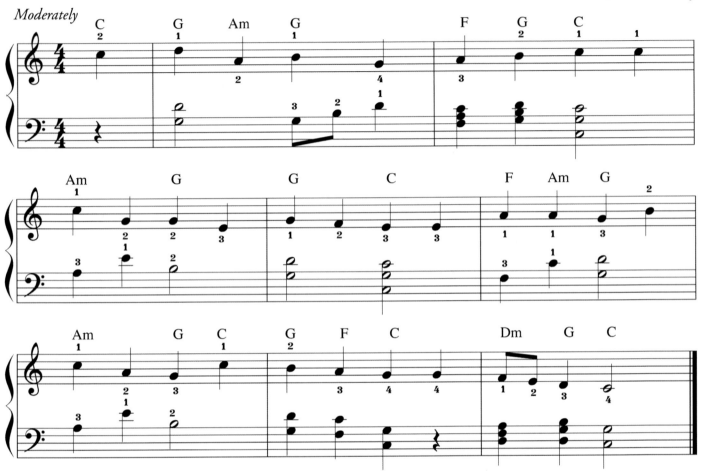

Vom Himmel hoch, da komm' ich her,
ich bring'euch gute neue Mär,
der guten Mär bring' ich so viel,
davon ich sing'n und sagen will.

Euch ist ein Kindlein heut' gebor'n
von einer Jungfrau, auserkor'n;
ein Kindelein so zart und fein,
das soll eu'r Freud' und Wonne sein.

Ach, mein herzliebes Jesulein,
mach dir ein rein sanft' Bettelein,
zu ruh'n in meines Herzens Schrein,
dass ich nimmer vergesse dein'.

—*Martin Luther, 1535*

From heaven above to earth I come
To bear good news to every home;
Glad tidings of great joy I bring,
Whereof I now will say and sing:

To you this night is born a Child
Born of a blessed virgin mild;
This little Child of lowly birth,
Shall be the joy of all the earth.

Ah, dearest Jesus, holy Child,
Make thee a bed, soft, undefiled,
Within my heart, that it may be
A quiet chamber kept for Thee.

—*English tr., Catherine Winkworth, 1855*

Green Grows the Holly

English, 16th Century, attributed to Henry VIII

Green grows the holly,
So does the ivy;
Though winter winds
Blow ne'er so high,
Green grow the holly

Green grows the holly,
So does the ivy;
The God of life can never die,
"Hope!" says the holly.

I Saw Three Ships

English/Cornish, 17th Century

I saw three ships come a-sailing in,
On Christmas Day, on Christmas Day,
I saw three ships come a-sailing in,
On Christmas Day in the morning.

And who was on those ships all three?
On Christmas Day, on Christmas Day,
And who was on those ships all three?
On Christmas Day, in the morning?

'Twas Joseph and his fair lady,
On Christmas Day, on Christmas Day,
'Twas Joseph and his fair lady,
On Christmas Day in the morning.

And he did whistle and she did sing,
On Christmas Day, on Christmas Day,
And he did whistle and she did sing,
On Christmas Day in the morning.

Pray, whither sailed those ships all three?
On Christmas Day, on Christmas Day,
Pray, whither sailed those ships all three?
On Christmas Day in the morning.

O, they sailed into Bethlehem,
On Christmas Day, on Christmas Day,
O, they sailed into Bethlehem,
On Christmas Day, in the morning.

And all the bells on earth shall ring,
On Christmas Day, on Christmas Day,
And all the angels in heaven shall sing,
On Christmas Day, on the morning.

And all the souls on earth shall sing,
On Christmas Day, on Christmas Day,
Then let us all rejoice amain!
On Christmas Day, on the morning.

—Cornish traditional, based on
12th Century Apocrypha

Joseph lieber, Joseph mein
Joseph Dearest, Joseph Mine

German, 14th Century

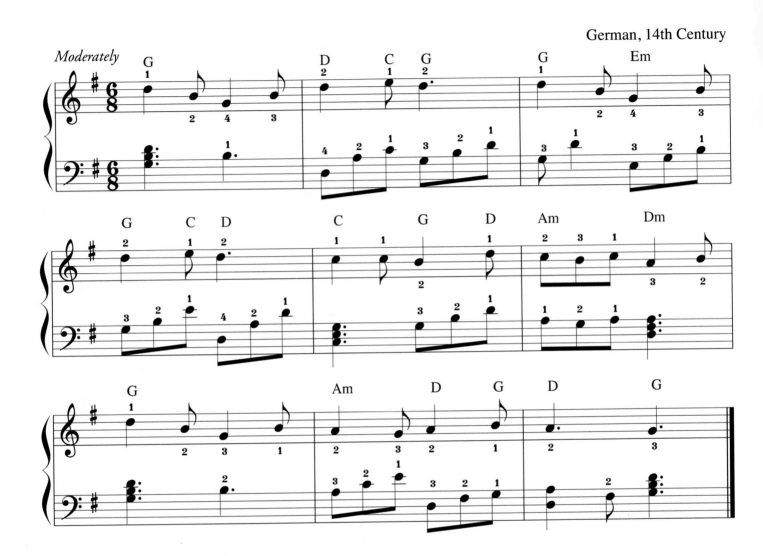

Joseph lieber, Joseph mein,
hilf mir wiegen mein Kindelein!
Gott, der wird mein Lohner sein
im Himmelreich, der Jungfrau's Sohn Maria.

Gerne, liebe Muhme mein,
helf' ich dir wiegen dein Kindelein!
Gott, dir wird mein Lohner sein
im Himmelreich, der Jungfrau's Kind Maria.

Joseph dearest, Joseph mine,
Help me rock the Child divine,
God reward both thee and thine,
In paradise, so prays the mother Mary.

I will gladly, lady mine,
Help thee rock the Child divine,
God's heavenly light on thee will shine,
In paradise, so prays the mother Mary.

—*German and English traditional*

Nous voici dans la ville

(In This Town of Bethlehem)

Sharp the G above middle C.

French, 15th Century

21

Nova! Nova!

Scottish, 15th Century

Nova, nova: 'Ave' fit ex 'Eva'.
Gabriel of high degree,
He came down from Trinity,
From Nazareth to Galilee.
Nova! Nova!
Nova! Nova: 'Ave' fit ex 'Eva'.

He met a maiden in a place,
And kneeléd down before her face,
He said "Hail Mary, full of grace."
Nova! Nova!
Nova! Nova: 'Ave' fit ex 'Eva'.

When the maiden heard tell of this,
She was full sore abashed I-wys,
And deemed she had done amiss.
Nova! Nova!
Nova! Nova: 'Ave' fit ex 'Eva'.

Then said the angel:
Dread not thou,
Ye shall conceive in all virtue
A child whose name shall be Jesu.
Nova! Nova!
Nova! Nova: 'Ave' fit ex 'Eva'.

Then said the maiden verely:
I am your servant right truly.
Ecce ancilla Domini.
Nova! Nova!
Nova! Nova: 'Ave' fit ex 'Eva'.

Note: Nova is the feminine form of the Latin word "new"; 'Ave' fit ex 'Eva' means Ave, as in Ave Maria, is the reverse of Eva, or Eve; and Ecce ancilla Domini translates as "behold the handmaiden of the Lord."

Orientis Partibus

Leave the F above middle C natural.

French, 12th Century

Orientus partibus
Adventavit asinus
Pulcher et fortissimus
Sarcinis aptissimus,
Hez, Sir Asne, hez.

Aurum de Arabia,
Thus et myrrham de Saba
Tulit in ecclesia
Virtus asinaria,
Hez, Sir Asne, hez.

Amen dicas, asine,
Iam satur de gramine,
Amen, amen itera,
Aspernare vetera,
Hez, Sir Asne, hez.

From Eastern lands
The donkey comes,
Beautiful and very strong,
Suited to great burdens,
Hail, Sir Ass, hail!

Gold he brings from Arabia,
Fragrant myrrh from Saba,
He bears them to the church
This Virtuous donkey,
Hail, Sir Ass, hail!

"Amen" you say, Ass,
Grazing your fill on sweet grass,
Amen, you say,
Your travels are ended,
Hail Sir Ass, hail!

Past Three o' Clock
Carol of the London Waits

Personent Hodie
On This Day

German/Bohemian, Piae Cantiones, 1582

Personent hodie
Voces puerulae
Laudantes iucunde
Qui nobis est natus,
Summo Deo datus,
Et de vir-, vir-, vir-,
Et de virgineo
  Ventre procreatus.

In mundo nascitur;
Pannis involvitur;
Praesepi ponitur
Stabulo brutorum
Rector supernorum;
Perdidit spolia
  Prencep Infernorum.

Magi tres venerunt;
Munera offerunt;
Parvulum inquirunt,
Stellulam sequendo,
Ipsum adorando,
Aurum, thus et myrrham
  Ei offerendo.

Omnes clericuli,
Pariter pueri,
Cantent ut angeli:
Advenisti mundo:
Laudes tibi fundo
Ideo: Gloria
  In excelsis Deo.

—*Piae Cantiones*, 1582

On this day earth shall ring
with the song children sing
to the Lord, Christ our King,
born on earth to save us;
him the Father gave us.
Ideo, Ideo,
Ideo gloria in excelsis Deo!

His the doom, ours the mirth;
when he came down to earth,
Bethlehem saw his birth;
ox and ass beside him
from the cold would hide him.
Ideo, Ideo,
Ideo gloria in excelsis Deo!

God's bright star, o'er his head,
Wise Men three to him led;
kneel they low by his bed,
lay their gifts before him,
praise him and adore him.
Ideo, Ideo,
Ideo gloria in excelsis Deo!

On this day angels sing;
with their song earth shall ring,
praising Christ, heaven's King,
born on earth to save us;
peace and love he gave us.
Ideo Ideo,
Ideo gloria in excelsis Deo!

—*Jane M. Joseph (1894–1929)*

Riu Riu Chiu

Riu riu chiu,
La guarda ribera;
Dios guardo el lobo
De nuestra cordera,
Dios guardo el lobo
De neustra cordera.

El lobo rabioso
La guiso morder,
Mas Dios poderoso
La supa defender;
Quisola hazer que
No pudises pecar,
Niaun original
Esta Virgen no tuviera.

Este qu'es naçido
Es el gran Monarcha,
Christo patriarca
De carne vestido;
Hemos redemido
Con se hazer chiquito,
Aunqu'era infinito,
Finito se hiziera.

Riu riu chiu,
Guardian of the river,
God has kept the wolf
From our lamb, our Lady.
God has kept the wolf
From our Lamb, our Lady.

Raging mad the wolf,
There he stole to bite her
But our God Almighty
Defended her with fervor
Pure He wished to keep her
She could never sin,
The first sin of man
Never touched the blessed Virgin.

He who is now born
Is our mighty Monarch,
Christ, our Lord divine,
In human flesh is clothed;
He has brought atonement
By being born so humble,
Though He is immortal,
As a mortal he has come.

The Seven Joys of Mary

English, 16th Century

The first good joy that Mary had, it was the joy of one;
To see the blessed Jesus Christ when He was first her Son.
When He was first her Son, good man, and joyful may we be,
Sing Father, Son and Holy Ghost, to all eternity.

The next good joy that Mary had, it was the joy of two;
To see her own Son Jesus Christ making the lame to go.
Making the lame to go, good man, and joyful may we be,
Sing Father, Son and Holy Ghost, to all eternity.

The next good joy that Mary had, it was the joy of three;
To see her own sweet Jesus Christ making the blind to see.
Making the blind to see, good man, and joyful may we be,
Sing Father, Son and Holy Ghost, to all eternity.

The next good joy that Mary had, it was the joy of four;
To see her own sweet Jesus Christ reading the Bible o'er.
Reading the Bible o'er, good man, and joyful may we be,
Sing Father, Son and Holy Ghost, to all eternity.

The next good joy that Mary had, it was the joy of five;
To see her own sweet Jesus Christ raising the dead to life.
Raising the dead to life, good man, and joyful may we be,
Sing Father, Son and Holy Ghost, to all eternity.

The next good joy that Mary had, it was the joy of six;
To see her own sweet Jesus Christ upon the crucifix.
Upon the crucifix, good man, and joyful may we be,
Sing Father, Son and Holy Ghost, to all eternity.

The next good joy that Mary had, it was the joy of seven;
To see her own sweet Jesus Christ ascending into heaven.
Ascending into heaven, good man, and joyful may we be,
Sing Father, Son and Holy Ghost, to all eternity.

Song of the Ship
Uns kommt ein Schiff

Andernach Gesanguch, 1608

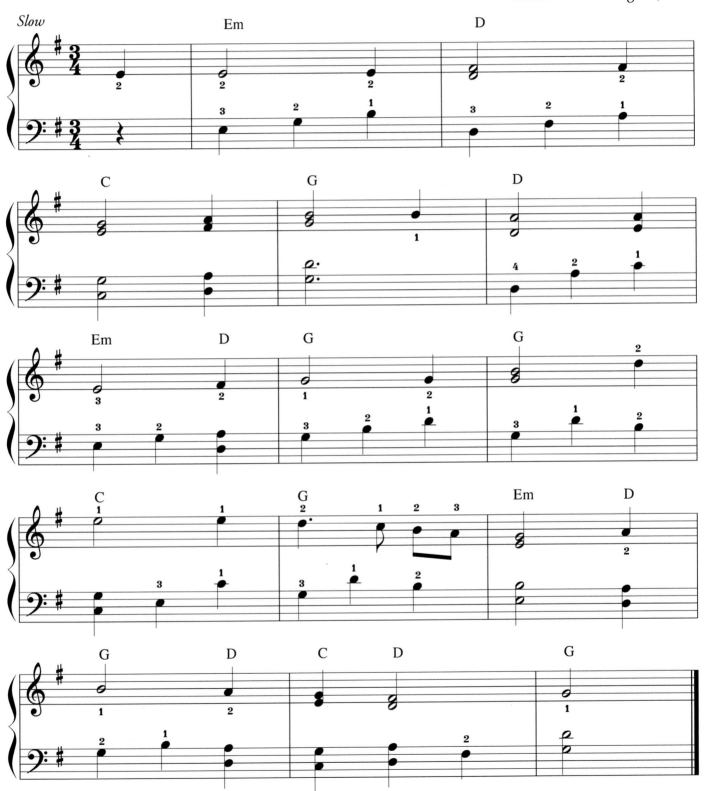

Es kommt ein Schiff, geladen
bis an sein' höchsten Bord,
trägt Gottes Sohn voll Gnaden,
des Vaters ewigs Wort.

Das Schiff geht still im Triebe,
es trägt ein teure Last;
das Segel ist die Liebe,
der Heilig Geist der Mast.

Der Anker haft' auf Erden,
da ist das Schiff am Land.
Das Wort will Fleisch uns werden,
der Sohn ist uns gesandt.

—Johannes Tauler, 1340

A silent ship comes sailing
With host of angels bright;
She bears a precious burden
As she sails through the night.

Now through the oceans stormy
The ship steers to the shore.
To bring mankind the riches
She holds within her store.

For this ship's name is Mary
Of flowers the rose is she.
She brings to us the Child
Whose love shall set men free.

This Endris Night
The Other Night

English, 15th Century

The other night I saw a sight,
A star as bright as day
And ever among
A maiden sang: Lully, by by, lully.

This virgin pure, without a peer,
Unto her son did say:
My Son, my Lord, my Father dear,
Why liest thou in hay?

Methink by right, that King and Knight
Should lie in rich array.
Yet never the less I will not cease
To sing by by, lullay

The Babe full spoke, and answer gave,
And thus I thought he said:
I am a King above all things,
In hay though I be laid;

The angels bright, round me shall light.
And guard me night and day:
And for that sight thou mays't delight
To sing by by, Lullay.

My mother sweet, when I must sleep,
Then take me up at last,
Upon your knee that you set me
and handle me full soft;

And in your arms hold me right warm,
And keep me night and day
And if I weep and cannot sleep,
Sing "by by lullay."

My Son, I say, and to thee pray,
Thou art my darling dear;
I shall thee keep, while thou dost sleep
And make the goodly cheer;

And all the while, I will fulfill,
Thou knowest well, in faith
Yet more than this,
I will thou kiss and sing by by lullay.

My Son, my Lord, my Father dear,
Since all is at thy will.
I pray thee, Son,
Grant me a boon, If it be right and skill:

To bliss thou bring,
And I shall sing, by by, lullay.
That child or man as may or can
Be merry on this day.

The other night I saw a sight,
A star as bright as day
And ever among
A maiden sang: Lully, by by, lully.

To Drive the Cold Winter Away
All Hayle to the Days

English, late 16th / early 17th Century

All hail to the days that merit more praise
Than all of the rest of the year,
And welcome the nights that double delights
As well for the poor as the peer!
Good fortune attend each merry man's friend
That doth but the best that he may,
Forgetting old wrongs with carols and songs
To drive the cold winter away.

This time of the year is spent in good cheer,
And neighbors together do meet,
To sit by the fire with friendly desire,
Each other in love to greet.
Old grudges forgot are put by the pot,
All sorrows aside they lay;
The old and the young doth carol this song,
To drive the cold winter away.

'Tis ill for a mind to anger inclined
To think of small injuries now;
If wrath be to seek, lend not her thy cheek,
Nor let her inhabit thy brow.
Cross out of thy books malevolent looks,
Both beauty and youth's decay,
And wholly consort with mirth and with sport,
To drive the cold winter away.

When Christmastide comes in like a bride,
With Holly and Ivy clad,
Twelve days of the year much mirth and good cheer
In every household is had;
The country guise is then to devise
Some gambol of Christmas play,
Where at the young men
Do the best that they can
To drive the cold winter away.

When white bearded Frost
Has threatened his worst
And fallen from branch and brier,
Then time away calls from husbandry halls
And from the good countryman's fire
Together to go to plow and to sow
To get us both food and array;
And thus with content the time we have spent
To drive the cold winter away.

Tomorrow Shall Be My Dancing Day

French, 17th Century

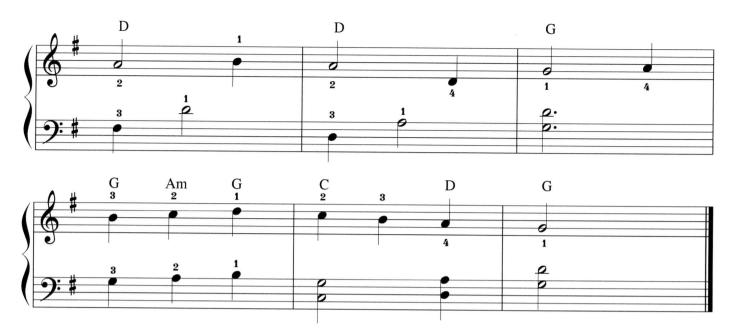

Tomorrow shall be my dancing day;
I would my true love
 Did so chance
To see the legend of my play,
To call my true love to the dance.
Sing O my love, O my love,
My love, my love, my love,
This have I done for my true love.

Then I was born of a virgin pure;
Of her I took my earthly substance.
Thus was I knit to man's nature,
To call my true love to the dance.
Sing O, etc.

In a manger laid and wrapped I was,
So very poor; this was my chance,
Betwixt the ox and a silly poor ass,
To call my true love to the dance.
Sing O, etc.

Then afterwards baptized I was;
The Holy Ghost on me did glance,
My Father's voice heard from above
To call my true love to the dance.
Sing O, etc.

Into the desert I was led,
Where I fasted without substance;
The devil bade me make stones my bread,
To have me break my true love's dance.
Sing O, etc.

For thirty pence Judas me sold,
His covetousness for to advance:
"Mark whom I kiss, the same do hold!"
The same is he shall lead the dance.
Sing O, etc.

Then on the cross hanged I was,
Where spear my heart did glance;
There issued forth my heart's own blood,
To call my true love to the dance.
Sing O, etc.

Then down to hell I did descend,
For my true love's deliverance,
And rose again on the third day,
Up to my true love and the dance.
Sing O, etc.

Then up to heaven I did ascend,
Where now I dwell in sure substance
On the right hand of God, that man
May come unto the general dance.
Sing O, etc.

—*English, traditional*

Veinticinco de Diciembre
Twenty-Fifth Day of December, or Fum, Fum, Fum

Sharp the G above middle C.

Spanish, 15th Century

Veintecinco de diciembre,
Fum, fum, fum!
Veinticinco de diciembre,
Fum, fum, fum!
Nacido ha por nuestro amor,
El Niño Dios, el Niño Dios
Hoy de la virgen Maria
En esta noche tan fria,
Fum, fum, fum!

Pajaritos del los bosques,
Fum, fum, fum!
Pajaritos de los bosques,
Fum, fum, fum!
Vuestros hijos de coral
Abandonad, abandonad,
Y formad un muelle nido
A Jesus recien nacido,
Fum, fum, fum!

Estrellitas de los cielos,
Fum, fum, fum!
Estrellitas de los cielos,
Fum, fum, fum!
Que a Jesu mirais llorar
Y no llordis, y no llordis,
Alumbrad la noche ascura
Con vuestra luz clara y pura,
Fum, fum, fum!

On December twenty-fifth sing
Fum, fum, fum!
On December twenty-fifth sing
Fum, fum, fum.
For a blessed Child was born
Upon this day at break of morn.
In a manger poor and lowly,
Lies the Son of God most Holy.
Fum, fum, fum!

—*Spanish and English, traditional*

Whence Comes This Rush of Wings?
Voici l'etoile de Nöel

Sharp the F above middle C.

Bas-Quercy, 17th Century

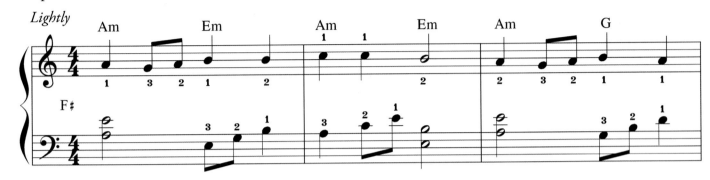

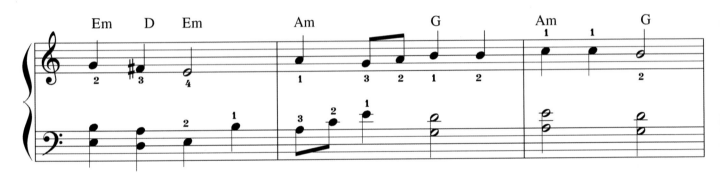

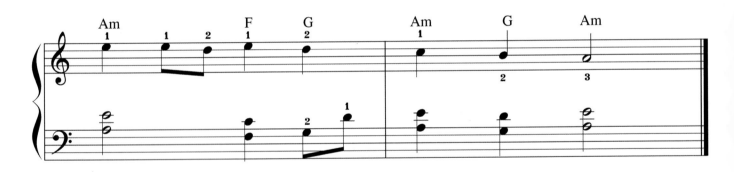

Voici l'étoile de Noël!
  Quel est ce bruit sur la maison?
  C'est une troupe d'oiselets,
  À Bethléhem vont deux á deux.

Dans l'étable oú le Roi du ceil
Dort entre l'âne et le boeuf brun,
Pourquoi venez-vous donc, oiseaux?
"Nous venons pour adorer Dieu!"

  Pour honorer le Fils De Dieu,
  Venez en grande dévotion,
  Anges, berges, oiseaux du ceil,
  Chantez Noël! Chantez Noël!

—*French traditional*

Whence comes this rush of wings afar,
Following straight the Noël star?
Birds from the woods in wondrous flight,
Bethlehem seeking this holy night.

"Tell us, O birds, why come ye here,
Into this stable, poor and drear?"
"Hast'ning we seek the new-born King,
And all our sweetest music bring."

Angels and shepherds, birds of the sky,
Come where the son of God doth lie;
Christ on earth with man doth dwell,
Join in the shout: Noël! Noël!

—English translation, traditional

While By My Sheep
Als Ich Meinen Schafen Wacht

German, 15th Century

Sharp the G above middle C as indicated in the next to last line.

While by my sheep, I watched at night,
Glad tidings brought an angel bright.

How great my joy! Great my joy!
Joy, joy, joy! Joy, joy, joy!
Praise we the Lord in heaven on high!

There shall be born, so did he say,
In Bethlehem a Child this day.

How great my joy! Great my joy!
Joy, joy, joy! Joy, joy, joy!
Praise we the Lord in heaven on high!

Go where he sleeps within a stall,
This Child who shall redeem us all.

How great my joy! Great my joy!
Joy, joy, joy! Joy, joy, joy!
Praise we the Lord in heaven on high!

The Child asleep in a manger lay,
There by His side longed I to stay.

How great my joy! Great my joy!
Joy, joy, joy! Joy, joy, joy!
Praise we the Lord in heaven on high!

This gift of God I'll cherish well,
That ever joy my heart shall fill.

How great my joy! Great my joy!
Joy, joy, joy! Joy, joy, joy!
Praise we the Lord in heaven on high!

—*English tr., traditional*

Notes on the Music

A Babe Is Born All of a Maid. A fifteenth century English Epiphany carol. This carol appears in the Sloane manuscript, which dates to the early part of the fifteenth century, and is believed to have been the song book of a minstrel. It is also in *Richard Hill's Commonplace Book*. Hill was a sixteenth century London grocer. His remarkable book was begun around 1500, and contains not only a number of carols, but poems in English, French and Latin, recipes for medicines and food, instructions for brewing beer and breaking horses, riddles, satires and reflections on life— all interspersed with laundry lists, the dates of numerous events and the birthdays of his children. His last entry is dated 1536.

Angelus ad Virginem. Chaucer mentions this carol in *The Canterbury Tales*, where it is sung by the clerk at the beginning of the Miller's Tale. The text of "Angelus ad Virginem" is attributed to Phillip the Chancellor (d. 1236).

Besançon Carol. This Advent noël from the Besançon region of France is included in the 1717 collection *La Clef des Chansonniers*, as one of the tunes more than a century old. It most likely dates to the late fifteenth century. The lyrics are probably eighteenth century, replacing the original text.

Corde Natus ex Parentis. The words of this hymn were written in the fourth century by the Roman-Spanish lawyer Aurelius Prudentius. In 1853 John Mason Neale set the text to the melody of "Divinum mysterium," a melody from a sixteenth century collection of songs called *Piae Cantiones*. This rare Scandinavian manuscript was compiled by a Theoderius Petrus around 1581, and contains a treasure trove of early music from many parts of Europe. Neale acquired the manuscript in 1852 and published two collections of arrangements and translations. The best known piece is "Tempus adest floridum," to which he set his own lyrics, creating the enduringly popular carol "Good King Wenceslas."

The Cutty Wren. The melody of this traditional Welsh wren song is believed to date to the fifteenth century. The ritual of hunting the wren on St. Stephen's Day (the day after Christ-mas) was at one time widespread throughout Ireland, Wales and the Island of Man. The custom is recorded in the Welsh manuscript *Llyfr Coch Hergest* (the red book of Hergest), from the period of 1375-1425.

Dadme Albricas, hijos d'Eva. "Reward my tidings, sons of Eve" A fifteenth century Spanish carol, or villancico, from the collection *Villancicos de diuersos Autores*, published in Venice in 1556. Many of the pieces in that collection came originally from the Valencian court.

From Heaven Above. Martin Luther wrote the words for this lovely hymn around 1535, He borrowed the melody from a Fifteenth century folk song. In Germany, the Reformation inspired a tremendous wealth of new Christmas music, Luther often adapted folk music, and encouraged the writing of new works.

The Friendly Beasts. A children's carol with its origins in the twelfth century, this charming piece is related to Orientis Partibus (page 24). The English words are often listed as traditional, but were actually written in the early twentieth century by Robert Davis (1881-1950).

Green Grows the Holly. This hauntingly lovely sixteenth century song is, like "Greensleeves," attributed (although, probably apocryphally) to Henry VIII.

I Saw Three Ships. I love the image of these magical ships sailing into the dusty land-bound town of Bethlehem. This is an enormously popular English carol that appears in many broadsides. The text refers to apocryphal legends popular in the twelfth century. Both the text, and the more common melody appear in Forbes's *Cantus* (c. 1666). This variation, which comes from Cornwall, has very much the feel of a Renaissance dance.

Joseph, Dearest Joseph Mine/Joseph, Lieber Joseph Mien. Also known as "Resonet in Laudibus," both the words and the text of this German song date to the early fourteenth century and are related to the medieval custom of rocking a cradle for the Christ Child during the Christmas mass. This song was also traditionally performed at weddings of that period, where it was accompanied by a vigorous dance.

Nous voici dans la ville. One of the best loved and most beautiful French noëls. The melody dates to at least 1450, and may be older.

Nova! Nova! This fifteenth century annunciation carol is a good example of a macaronic carol, a carol combining Latin and vernacular. "Ave fit ex Eva" is a medieval play on words referring to the popular medieval belief that Mary, in accepting the angel's request, had redeemed Eve and therefore all women. The dance-like tune originates in Scotland.

Orientis Partibus. This humorous twelfth century conductus, or Latin lyric poem, with its refrain of braying, celebrates the humble donkey. Originally part of the liturgical plays performed at Beauvais, it was sung while a live donkey was ridden, with great pageantry, into the cathedral.

Past Three o'Clock. During the medieval period many towns and cities employed a civilian town watch, or wait, to patrol the town and sounded the hours. Each town's waits had a unique "signature tune" for their call. By the seventeenth century the waits had become civic musicians instead of watchmen, performing for the public and, in later years, traveling from door to door singing to bring luck. This piece is based on the hourly call of the London city waits. Playford records the melody in *The English Dancing Master*, published in 1665.

Personent Hodie (On this Day). Most likely written during the early fourteenth century to celebrate Holy Innocents Day (generally celebrated on December 28), "Personent Hodie" is preserved in Theoderius Petrus's famous sixteenth century collection of songs *Piae Cantiones*.

Riu Riu Chiu. A Spanish carol dating from the fifteenth century. It is among the pieces in *Villancicos de diversos Autores*. "Riu riu chiu" is thought to have been the traditional cry of the Spanish shepherds.

Seven Joys of Mary. A tremendously popular English ballad with many versions. The Sloane Manuscript give five joys, beginning with: "The ferste joye, as I you tell: When Mary met Seynt Gabrielle..." The number of joys has increased over time, and later broadside versions list as many as ten or twelve. The Joys were once part of medieval religious devotion, and are thought to have evolved from the same traditions as the Rosary. The practice of celebrating the Joys fell out of favor during the Reformation.

Song of the Ship. Another song with nautical imagery, this time from Germany. The text is attributed to the fourteenth century German mystic Johannes Tauler. The melody is preserved in the 1608 collection of songs *Andernach Gesangbuch*. My father, John Guldimann, helped me to create an English version that fits the music. This carol always makes me think of him.

This Endris Night. A strange and visionary English carol from the early Fifteenth century. This Endris Night can be found in a number of fifteenth and sixteenth century manuscripts, including the Hill MS. "endris night," translates as "the other night" or "a few nights ago."

To Drive the Cold Winter Away. This piece appears on an early seventeenth century broad-side in the collection of Samuel Pepys, although the ballad itself dates to the mid sixteenth century. There is a related piece in Playford's English Dancing Master. The first verse given here is later, attributed to Tom Durfey, the playwright to Charles II. There are actually few seventeenth century English carols. The Reformation, which in Germany had inspired a new interest in Christmas music, in England led to a repressive puritanism that frowned on song and celebration. Christmas Day was "abolished" by Cromwell's Parliament in 1644. The ban lasted for sixteen years. The Christmas carol did not regain favor until the start of the nineteenth century, and by then many songs and traditions were lost.

Tomorrow Shall Be My Dancing Day. This is a true carol, with it's roots in the ancient French carole, a circular dance accompanied by song. The text recounts the entire life of Christ, a popular theme in medieval "prophecy" carols.

Veinticino de Diciembre. In America this is probably the best known Spanish carol. It has it's origins as a medieval song dance. The refrain of "fum, fum, fum" is said to imitate the beating of the tambor, or drum, originally played to keep time in the dance.

Whence Comes This Rush of Wings? A wondrous flight of wild birds greet the Christ Child in this beautiful seventeenth century noël from the Bas-Quency region of France.

While by My Sheep. A fifteenth century carol from the ancient cathedral city of Trier, in the Rhine province of Germany. This carol may once have been part of a medieval mystery-play, the echo in the refrain sung from off stage.

Harp music books by SUZANNE GULDIMANN

GREEN GROWS the HOLLY:
Medieval & Renaissance Christmas Carols

THE THREE RAVENS
& Other Ballads

COLD DECEMBER WINDS
A New Collection of Old Carols

PASTIME with GOOD COMPANY
Elizabethan Songs & Dances

HEARTS of OAK:
Songs & Dances of Old England

AMID the WINTER SNOW
Victorian Christmas Carols

THE KING'S DELIGHT
A Collection of Early Music

THE BARD'S HARP
Songs & Dances from Shakespeare's Plays

MUSIC for the NETHERFIELD BALL
Songs & Dances of Jane Austen's Era

WEST OF THE MOON BOOKS
Malibu, California
www.westofthemoon.org

Made in the USA
Middletown, DE
05 September 2024